W9-BYZ-044

A+ books

Shapes around Town

# Rectangles
## around Town

by Nathan Olson

Capstone press®

Mankato, Minnesota

A+ Books are published by Capstone Press,
151 Good Counsel Drive, P.O. Box 669, Mankato, Minnesota 56002.
www.capstonepress.com

1 2 3 4 5 6 11 10 09 08 07 06

*Library of Congress Cataloging-in-Publication Data*
Olson, Nathan.
    Rectangles around town / by Nathan Olson.
    p. cm.—(A+ books. Shapes around town)
    Summary: "Simple text, photographs, and illustrations help readers identify rectangles that can be found in
a city"—Provided by publisher.
    Includes bibliographical references and index.
    ISBN-13: 978-0-7368-6370-4 (hardcover)
    ISBN-10: 0-7368-6370-2 (hardcover)
    1. Rectangles—Juvenile literature. 2. Shapes—Juvenile literature. I. Title. II. Series.
QA482.O469 2007
516'.154—dc22                                                                          2006002952

**Credits**
Jenny Marks, editor; Kia Adams, designer; Renée Doyle, illustrator; Kelly Garvin, photo researcher/photo editor

**Photo Credits**
Corbis/Alan Schein Photography, 4–5; David Sailors, 12; Doug Wilson, 20–21; Elizabeth Whiting
    & Associates, 8; John and Lisa Merrill, 10; Louis K. Meisel Gallery, Inc., 18; Michael S. Yamashita, 14;
    Richard Cummins, 11; zefa/Fabio Cardoso, 15
Getty Images Inc./Stone/Daniel Bosler, 16–17
Image Farm, Inc., 26–27 (all)
Jake Smith/Jakobie.com, 23
Masterfile/Gail Mooney, 22
Photodisc, cover
Shutterstock/Danger Jacobs, 13; James E. Hernandez, 6
SuperStock/age fotostock, 9; Richard Cummins 7, 19, 24–25

**Note to Parents, Teachers, and Librarians**
The Shapes around Town set uses color photographs and a nonfiction format to introduce readers to
the shapes around them. *Rectangles around Town* is designed to be read aloud to a pre-reader, or
to be read independently by an early reader. Images and activities help early readers and listeners
perceive and recognize shapes. The book encourages further learning by including the following
sections: Table of Contents, Which Are Rectangles?, Welcome to Rectangle Town, Glossary, Read
More, Internet Sites, and Index. Early readers may need assistance using these features.

# Table of Contents

# What Is a Rectangle?

Rectangles are shapes with two long sides and two short sides. Let's find rectangles all around town.

A rectangle has four sides and
four corners. Two sides are long
and two sides are short.

Squares have four sides, too.
But each side is exactly the
same size.

# Everyday Rectangles

Brick houses are made of lots of little rectangles. The doors and windows are rectangles, too.

Have you ever heard a rectangle ring? You can make a call with this row of rectangles.

Fruits and vegetables fit side by side in rectangles at the market. Which is your favorite?

# Can you find little rectangles hidden inside big rectangles?

# Rectangles on the Move

Big cities have railway cars called trams. There's plenty to see through big rectangle windows.

Rectangle signs help people find their way through the city. Red signs tell you what is not allowed.

SNOW ROUTE
NO STANDING
DURING
EMERGENCY
VEHICLES TOWED

STOP
HERE ON
RED
SIGNAL
DEPT OF TRANSPORTATION

NO STANDING
ANYTIME

CENTRAL PARK
WEST
KEEP RIGHT
DEPT OF TRANSPORT

CENTRAL PARK
SOUTH

COLUMBU

ONE WAY

Basketballs are round, but the court is one big rectangle. Do you see more rectangle shapes nearby?

City playgrounds have plenty of fun rectangles. Hang around and count them.

School bus windows have two short sides and two long sides. How many kids are looking at you through rectangles?

Ready for shopping? You'll find plenty of rectangles for sale in big store windows.

Greenhouse walls are made of glass rectangles. Glass walls let the sunlight in.

The American flag is a rectangle.
It's called the "Stars and Stripes."

This rectangle fountain shows a different face every five minutes!

A certain building in the city holds hundreds of rectangles all neatly arranged on shelves. Do you know what it is called?

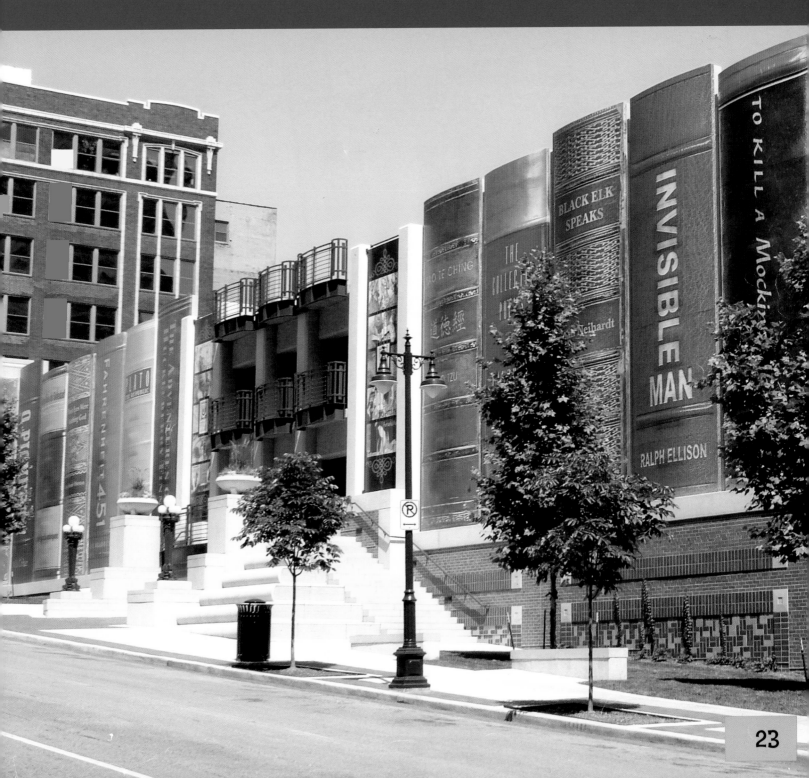

Rectangles give shape to cities all around the world. How many rectangles can you find in the city?

# Which Are Rectangles?

Rectangles are shapes with two long sides and two short sides. Which signs are rectangles?

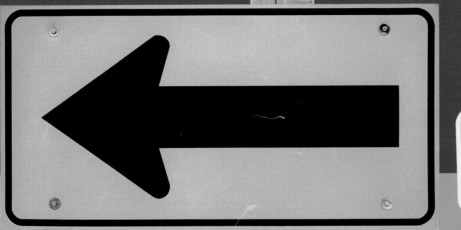

# Glossary

basketball court (BAS-kit-bawl KORT)—a flat area where basketball games are played

fountain (FOUN-tuhn)—a stream or spray of water used for decoration

greenhouse (GREEN-houss)—a warm building where plants can grow

tram (TRAM)—a public transportation vehicle that moves on a special pathway